Garfield
In The Fast Lane

JIM DAVIS

D1352421

RAVETTE BOOKS

Copyright © 1991
United Feature Syndicate, Inc.
All Rights Reserved
GARFIELD Comic Strips © 1989
United Feature Syndicate, Inc.

First published by
Ravette Books Limited 1991

_____

This book is sold subject to the condition that
it shall not, by way of trade or otherwise, be
lent, resold, hired out or otherwise circulated
without the publisher's prior consent in any
form of binding or cover other than that in
which this is published and without a similar
condition including this condition being
imposed on the subsequent purchaser.

Printed and bound in Great Britain
for Ravette Books Limited,
3 Glenside Estate, Star Road, Partridge Green,
Horsham, West Sussex RH13 8RA
by Cox & Wyman Ltd, Reading

ISBN 1 85304 330 3

© 1989 United Feature Syndicate, Inc.

7-4

© 1989 United Feature Syndicate, Inc.

JUST WHAT IS SUCCESS? TO SOME IT'S WEALTH AND NOTORIETY... TO SOME IT'S A SIMPLE SENSE OF SELF-WORTH, BUT TO ME IT'S CONTRIBUTING SOMETHING TOWARD THE BETTERMENT OF MANKIND

WHAT'S YOUR DEFINITION OF SUCCESS, GARFIELD?

JIM DAVIS 7-7

© 1989 United Feature Syndicate, Inc.

BEING ABLE TO EAT 20 PIZZAS WITHOUT THROWING UP

WHATEVER YOU SAID, I'M SURE WE ALL SAW THAT ONE COMING

© 1989 United Feature Syndicate, Inc.

HEY, GARFIELD! WE'RE GOING TO THE FARM TODAY!

FINE, I'LL BE OUTSIDE...

© 1989 United Feature Syndicate, Inc.

LETTING THE AIR OUT OF YOUR TIRES

JIM DAVIS

7-10

LUNCH, GARFIELD!

DON'T TOUCH HIM OR YOU'LL LOSE MY PAGE

7-20

© 1989 United Feature Syndicate, Inc.

© 1989 United Feature Syndicate, Inc.

© 1989 United Feature Syndicate, Inc.

© 1989 United Feature Syndicate, Inc.

© 1989 United Feature Syndicate, Inc.

7-28

© 1989 United Feature Syndicate, Inc.

© 1989 United Feature Syndicate, Inc.

8-4

© 1989 United Feature Syndicate, Inc.

© 1989 United Feature Syndicate, Inc.

SCREEEEEEEEE

THONK

© 1989 United Feature Syndicate, Inc.

JIM DAVIS 8-16

© 1989 United Feature Syndicate, Inc.

JIM DAVIS 9-1

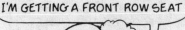

© 1989 United Feature Syndicate, Inc.

© 1989 United Feature Syndicate, Inc.

9-18 JIM DAVIS

© 1989 United Feature Syndicate, Inc.

9-27

© 1989 United Feature Syndicate, Inc.

© 1989 United Feature Syndicate, Inc.

JIM DAVIS   9-29

© 1989 United Feature Syndicate, Inc.

© 1989 United Feature Syndicate, Inc.

JIM DAVIS

10-9

© 1989 United Feature Syndicate, Inc.

© 1989 United Feature Syndicate, Inc.

JUST RIGHT!

© 1989 United Feature Syndicate, Inc.

JIM DAVIS

10-12

VERY FUNNY, GARFIELD!
YOU CAN'T MAKE ME
THINK YOUR
TEDDY BEAR
CAN SKATE!

© 1989 United Feature Syndicate, Inc.

SAY
AGAIN?

JIM DAVIS

10-14

© 1989 United Feature Syndicate, Inc.

© 1989 United Feature Syndicate, Inc.

© 1989 United Feature Syndicate, Inc.

AFTER YEARS OF TAKING LIFE FOR GRANTED, GARFIELD IS SHAKEN BY A HORRIFYING VISION OF THE INEVITABLE PROCESS CALLED "TIME"

HE HAS ONLY... ONE WEAPON...

DENIAL...

I DON'T WANT TO BE ALONE

WANT SOME BREAKFAST, GARFIELD?

© 1989 United Feature Syndicate, Inc.

WHO NEEDS IT? I NEED YOU!

10-28

AN IMAGINATION IS A POWERFUL TOOL. IT CAN TINT MEMORIES OF THE PAST, SHADE PERCEPTIONS OF THE PRESENT, OR PAINT A FUTURE SO VIVID THAT IT CAN ENTICE... OR TERRIFY, ALL DEPENDING UPON HOW WE CONDUCT OURSELVES TODAY... END

© 1989 United Feature Syndicate, Inc.

10-30

© 1989 United Feature Syndicate, Inc.

JPM DAV95 11-7

OTHER GARFIELD BOOKS IN THIS SERIES

LANDSCAPE SERIES

COLOUR TV SPECIALS

Here Comes Garfield	£2.95
Garfield On The Town	£2.95
Garfield In The Rough	£2.95
Garfield In Disguise	£2.95
Garfield In Paradise	£2.95
Garfield Goes To Hollywood	£2.95
A Garfield Christmas	£2.95
Garfield's Thanksgiving	£2.95

COLOUR TREASURIES

The Second Garfield Treasury	£5.95
The Third Garfield Treasury	£5.95
The Fourth Garfield Treasury	£5.95
The Fifth Garfield Treasury	£5.95
Garfield A Weekend Away	£4.95
Garfield Book Of Cat Names	£2.50
Garfield Best Ever	£4.95
Garfield The Easter Bunny?	£3.95
Garfield How To Party	£3.95
Garfield Selection	£5.95
Garfield His 9 Lives	£5.95

All these books are available at your local bookshop or newsagent, or can be ordered direct from the publisher. Just tick the titles you require and fill in the form below. Prices and availability subject to change without notice.

Ravette Books Limited, 3 Glenside Estate, Star Road, Partridge Green, Horsham, West Sussex RH13 8RA

Please send a cheque or postal order and allow the following for postage and packing. UK: Pocket-books – 45p for one book, 20p for a second book and 15p for each additional book. Landscape Series – 50p for one book plus 30p for each additional book. TV Specials and Cat Names – 45p for one book plus 30p for each additional book. Other titles – 85p for one book plus 50p for each additional book ordered.

Name ....

Address ....

....